Nathan Perelman

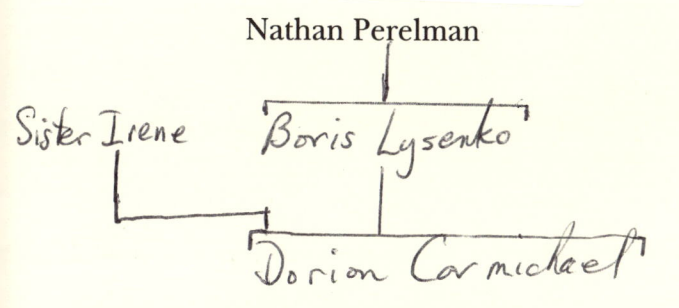

Sister Irene Boris Lysenko

Dorion Carmichael

Autumn Leaves

H.A. Frager & Co
Washington, D.C

Nathan Perelman
AUTUMN LEAVES

Translated from Russian by Henry Orlov
Edited by Joanne Hoover

Copyright © 1994 by Nathan Perelman
All rights reserved

Printed by Braun-Brumfield, Inc.
100 N. Staebler Road, Ann Arbor
Michigan 48106

ISBN 0-929647-06-8

A word from the author

The author is a pianist and a piano teacher. Offering these notes to the reader's judgement, he admits having no scientific aspirations whatsoever.

The author deems it necessary —

to vindicate himself in the eyes of sophisticated consumers of serious instructive writings by saying that he has had no intentions to be serious or systematic;

to warn credulous readers of their right to disagree with the author;

to inform strict critics that contradictions plentiful in these notes were unavoidable; they show how the author seeks the truth and how often it escapes him.

Those who prefer reading books from the end or from any other place will find in these notes assorted treasures while giving to the author a convenient chance to make the reader himself responsible for their inconsistencies.

Whatever the case, this little book is recommended for homeopathic consumption and unhurried digestion.

Nathan Perelman

It is easy to extract a necessary word from a stream of thoughts; it is much more difficult to extract a necessary thought from a stream of words.

When practicing at home spare your feelings, make your mind generous, and your hearing merciless.

Every morning sitting yourself down at the piano, pray to the long-drawn tone. Here is the text of the prayer:

and so on till the end of the octave. Especially zealous sound-worshippers may read it in reverse.

Advice to young musicians

Work six days, on the seventh day play, play, play.

Sing not *at* the piano, but *on* the piano.

Accompany to yourself not louder than to your nearest neighbor.

Don't steal from the record.

Don't use the pedal indiscriminately.

Don't whisper because even your nearest neighbor wouldn't hear you.

Be superstitious: fear underworked pieces.

Love polyphony from your early years, then in your old age it will serve you faithfully.

Don't invent pre-concert habits.

Coming for a concert, bring the music not in a suitcase but in your head.

Love your doings lightly and joyfully.

Precepts

1) When difficult — do by rote.

2) Doubt not until all the forms of the doubtless have been studied and analyzed.

3) For a committee play right.

4) Don't memorize the pedalling like the multiplication table.

5) Memorize the fingering like the multiplication table.

Don't spoil the joy of the child's morning meeting with the piano by the 'porridge of scales.' Let him first play something he loves; after that the scales will come out better.

It is possible to learn a piece without studying it, but it is impossible to have studied a piece without learning it.

To work through a new piece well is to disassemble it knowingly; after that it comes together easily. To work through a piece badly is to break it down thoughtlessly; fractured, it resists reintegration.

Don't bring a new piece to the lesson already memorized: I want to see how you look at the music.

Ability to read and execute music belongs to the pre-artistic sphere; the sphere of the artistic begins with interpretation.

Beware of skills turning into habits. That which does not change rots.

Repetition without accumulation — step-mother of learning.

An artist is only he who in the desert of notes envisions a mirage.

Graduate the key and the pedal, for the tone responds to your touch like mercury to the temperature.

To a musician, the sound is a creature that has a certain taste, color, volume, beauty or ugliness, strength, weight, length and everything that a musician with imagination is capable of putting into it. Notice: the musician with no fear of being ridiculous describes the sound as if it were a fruit — succulent, soft, tender; something visible — luminous, dull, sunny, bleak, white; an object with a volume, weight and length — round, flat, deep, shallow, heavy, light, long, short. The sound is even described in moral terms: noble.

On Passages

Fast passages have to be 'spoken.' Having grasped and fallen in love with the contents of a passage, it becomes embarrassing to run past them.

A Chopin's fast passage contains enough melodic material for five or six Nocturnes. Having understood this, you will not take it lightly.

Fortissimo of a fast passage is achieved by 98% *piano* and 2% *mezzo forte,* multiplied by the speed.

Even in the desperate cry 'disaster!' only one syllable 'AAH' yells in *ff*, while all the others abide in *piano*. Fast passages with a 'desperate dynamics' marked *ff* should follow the same redeeming rule.

The most important thing in fluidity is evenness; the most difficult, slowing down.

On the Texture

Talented inarticulate playing differs from giftless inarticulate playing as rich rags differ from poor rags.

Absolute synchronicity of the voices is mandated in polyphony. Synchronicity of rhythmic, harmonic and melodic supports is sufficient to guard homophony from laxity and vulgarity. Here attempts to play everything synchronically give the performance the expression of a tetanus sufferer.

An ABC of polyphony is synchronicity of the voices; its complexity lies in asynchronicity of their behaviors.

Mediocre execution of all the texture's coordinated elements should be preferred over the flawless performance of a single, even the most important element, with inattention to the rest. The former can be developed to perfection, the latter — never.

Sudden amplifications of subordinate elements, unusually slow or fast tempos are unhealthy symptoms of innovation itch.

The teacher-performer should not abuse the verb 'to stress.' By stressing something we give it preference. But in the arts everything is preferable; here 'small deeds' do not exist. Isn't the verb 'distribute' better? It doesn't imply preference to anything yet facilitates establishing of the best relationships. At the lessons of 'sound distribution' the teacher should liken himself to a sound-recording engineer: calmly and matter-of-factly move the levers of the pupil's hearing attention.

The innermost sense of a composition is hidden in the web of texture like a berry in the grass. Search for it carefully lest you squash it.

Remaking of the texture is forbidden; refitting it to make it more comfortable is permitted.

On Intonation

The art of intonation has to be practiced like that of leaps, octaves, trills etc. I dream of a collection of Etudes with such titles as No 1 — Etude questioning, No 3 — Etude of surprise, No 4 — Etude of grief etc, etc. Two books each containing 24 such Etudes would serve only as sparks which, however, will ignite imagination.

Rhythm enslaves intonation, the pulse liberates it. 'Quantity' of a tempo allows change, 'character' of a tempo does not.

The ability of intonation to transform the length of a note is amazing. An imperative one can melt a sixteenth into a thirty-secondth, while a submissive one can cool it into an eighth.

Truly, there is a sadder story in the world — concerto by Mozart. On the page it looks like the face of a clock. It is elementary — it counts time away: the quarter — the hour hand, the eighth — the minute hand, the sixteenth — the second hand. That's all... But somewhere, within every notated time interval, hidden and inaccessible to notation lives the myriad of trembling, jubilating and mourning temporal particles-molecules of this most sorrowful story in the world, and perhaps the whole essence lies in them?! Maestro, how are you going to conduct — on one, on three, on six?

Expressive plasticity of intonation in Chopin's fast Etudes is often sacrificed to two tyrants: the tempo and the accent.

Chopin's Mazurkas are confessional. However, this does not oblige us incessantly and fervently to cross ourselves with the mazurka rhythm.

'Don't whisper us,' plead Chopin's Mazurkas.

On the Left Pedal

The left pedal — a narcotic. Its excessive use — an addiction. It leads into a world of phantom sound, puts controls to sleep and develops into an ineradicable habit.

The sordino of the strings is like to our left pedal. Fortunately, the necessity every time to withdraw it (the sordino) out of the vest pocket reasonably limits its use. But where should we hide the left pedal?

I repeat three times and now with no hesitation: kick the harmful habit of clinging to the left pedal; you will immediately appreciate the gain.

Witchcraft in the arts is unpunishable.

* * *

Sometimes pupils 'plough away' on only the narrow spot on the surface of the white keys close to the edge, whereas using the whole virgin expanse of the key yields an excellent harvest.

The pianist's hand has six fingers: 1-2-3 and 3-4-5. The former are heavy yet free, the latter — light yet fettered. The 3rd finger is two-faced: in the first instance it is free, in the second — dependent. In order for the fingers to play evenly, the heavy ones should touch lighter, and the light ones heavier.

The best results can be achieved by relentlessly demanding from the pupil the impossible: *vibrato! pizzicato! Tutti! Corno! Drum!* Sing! Quartet! Clarinet!.. until the pupil starts having hallucinations of timbres and colors. Then it is done.

Everything that is good in the treasury of the performing art on any instrument and on any combination of instruments can and should be usurped by the piano.

Associations with orchestra and constant reminders of the orchestra's and quartet's exploits are born not out of a humble acceptance of their superiority, but out of the proud awareness that all those feats are within reach of our solitary piano.

Once more I suddenly found that yesterday in class I gave to the student who played Beethoven's Sonata

No 26 only one suggestion which I kept repeating during the entire lesson. I reiterated: '*tenuto*' and nothing else. But this *tenuto* entailed a host of unspoken yet carried out instructions.

Still I can't comprehend what prevails in our business — rules or exceptions; the moment I draw a rule I collide with an exception.

In class play two-hand pieces with the student with four hands: there is no better proof of the pianist's two-hand deficiency. Having tasted the sweetness of the four-handedness, the ear will expect double from every performer.

One can deceive the listener by an imposing performance of the sonata Allegros, assumed seriousness in Adagios, false grace in Scherzos, but in a Rondo it will misfire, for a lie repeated many times sooner or later betrays itself.

Am I not abusing the words 'joy,' 'pleasure,' 'love' in these notes? Where are then the proverbial 'ordeals of creation'? Well, these are nonexistent: through an oversight one word has been simply dropped; we should say: 'joyous ordeals of creation.'

Performer's doubts as to the priority of the right or the left hand in Chopin's Etudes are easily resolved:

play the 24 Etudes with each hand separately — you will have 48 complete works. This is a phenomenal circle: it divides and multiplies itself.

The time will come when improbably impeccable recording are replaced by recording with preconceived imprecisions simulating live performance. But nothing will ever replace the genuine truth of real stage spontaneity.

The artist's supreme virtue is not to submit to the composer's will but to detect, select and organize those of the composer's ideas which respond to the performer's strivings, peculiarities and capacities.

In the arts it is impossible to be loved by everyone. Great artists have possessed a tremendous force not only of attraction but also of repulsion.

Strengths and weaknesses of a performance show in *piano;* in *forte* they are easer to cover up.

A short slur differs from a long one only in that it is shorter — nothing else. Encountering it, violinists have to alternate the direction of the bow more frequently, and pianists have to use an appropriate fingering.

From a review: 'The famous American pianist has heightened charm.'

Ah, how difficult it is to master Mozart's lightness!

Development of taste is a process of subtraction, not addition.

Perhaps, one should not argue about tastes, but is it absolutely imperative to argue about the taste.

An excess of stage fright easily dissolves in these two states: 1) chronic delight with the music being performed, and 2) temporary rapture with oneself.

Self-criticism on the stage is the saw cutting off the legs of the pianist's bench.

On the stage you may err but not correct errors.

* * *

I understand César Franck's sufferings in 'Prelude, Chorale, and Fugue' and in 'Symphonic Variations' and feel compassion but am unable to help.

Having made the first step in the ascend to Mount Everest, don't act as if you have already reached it's peak... Don't lose you breath in the Introduction to Mozart's *Fantasia* in D: too early — you are still down below.

Left hand! In moments difficult for the right hand do not revel in the rests, collect yourself!

If on the stage you are swamped with artistic flabbiness, immediately electrify your left hand and order both hands to act absolutely synchronically.

Don't cut the music with the bar lines.

Had mankind treated the meridians on the globe as we treat bar lines, movements on our planet would have become rather difficult.

In the arts a simple problem is often more difficult to solve than a tough one.

To the gifted everything is easy, to the talented everything is difficult.

The harmony is the melody's mind, the modulation its action.

Recall the first measures of Chopin's Sonata in B minor: there is here a modulation from E–flat Major to G minor in a fast passage motion. The fingers could play it impeccably, and the ear could perceive it, but... if the heart has not noticed it, know — there was no modulation.

Only to hear the harmonic and modulatory life of a composition is the same as only to see a fragrant garden.

All the best qualities of sound combined have little value if they do not include the quality of magical attraction. One can attempt to get the purest feeling of a performer's concentrated 'sounding will' and, having achieved this, to develop it through the following exercises:

Exercise No 1: a) taking the first chord of Beethoven's *Concerto* in G, strive to achieve complete simultaneity of all of its eight notes; b) calmly repeating this chord with the pedal, make it ever softer until you reach the least audible volume with absolutely no losses (all the eight notes and on any piano). Never blame the piano for the losses: blame only yourself.

Exercise No 2: repeat the preceding precisely in your mind keeping the same tension in the fingers — as if playing on an 'air cushion' above the keyboard, but using the real pedal. Here, too, there should be no losses.

Exercise No 3: repeat all that with the four initial measures of the *Concerto* (in each of the first two measures there are four quiet touchings of the pedal).

Exercise No 4: Repeat the preceding mentally without losses and with the real pedal.

Preserve and treasure that life-saving corner of silliness that relishes in performing work torturous for the developed mind.

On Melody

A melodic line performed without intervalic tension is like lifeless posts to which someone forgot to attach high-voltage wires.

The voltage of tensions between the intervals is the most important element of the composer's style. Don't connect Mozart to the high-voltage circuit of Brahms: it will burn out.

If melodic gravitation had acted like Earth's gravitation — i.e., without the will of the attracted — music teachers would have been freed of a host of concerns.

It is impossible to imagine a normal person who in the word 'good' would pronounce only the consonants — 'g d.' But in the classroom we often hear musical similes of this 'g d.' And this is 'b d'!

'Legato' wouldn't spoil a piece, but 'staccato' should be strictly measured.

Excessive staccato makes Haydn and Mozart silly; excessive legato weakens them. Appropriate use of these devices does not save from all ails, but guards against at least these two.

Legato is not an articulation feature, but a state. Articulation starts with *portamento* and ends with *pizzicato*: one can't go any further.

All the features of articulation on the piano must be implemented, but legatos should be confessed.

It may appear that *tenuto* and *legato* have the same aim — binding. Yet the binding has different qualities. The former is aimed at independence of every sound, while the latter at subordination of the weak to the strong.

For all the instruments *tenuto* means action; only on the piano it appears as inaction behind which, however, hides an intense inner dynamics of hearing, attention, and control.

Tenuto is aggressive! Using the right of the strong one, it steals particles of time from neighboring weaker notes.

More on the Pedal

Love the pedal, study it, learn it, learn with it! Learn to pile on and peel off the pedal. The pedal is a cloud of sound and one feels like to speak about it as if it were a cloud — layered, fleecy, shrouding, overhanging, thunderous, floating, somber, light, bright! Instead we define it as 'dirty' or 'clean.'

One never loses touch with the pedal, for it is omnipresent like the air. Like the air, it can be thick, light, heavy, transparent, burning, suffused with fragrance, sterilly pure or barely perceptible, but it cannot be totally absent.

The pedal requires clever, not fastidious, ears.

Accompaniment in Mozart is like the bottom of a clear deep lake. Do not disturb it with the pedal. Light pedal ripples in the melody, independent finger suspensions in the broken harmonies guard the purity and flutter of Mozart's amazing speech.

The pedal is a cloud controlled by elemental forces of music and not a watering device with a thin hose of harmony which fails at every defenseless rest.

The pedal should be not a timid slave of harmony but its daring ally.

The proverbial 'touch' of the hands loses all its meaning if it is not extended to the legs!

From the youngest age pupils should be taught not only how to use pedal; they must fall in love with the pedal for with fingers alone they wouldn't attain artistic heights.

Staccato senza pedale on the piano is a caricature on *pizzicato* of the strings. A little bit of *con pedale,* and articulation acquires dignity.

Some believe that *staccato* and all the varieties of rests (and they are many) are doomed to cope without the pedal. The pedal drought afflicts mostly the classics, first of all Beethoven. Examples: Sonata No 10, Rondo in G, II movement of Sonata No 27 and many more.

The negative term 'lagging pedal' is bad, deficient. The pedal has to be timely.

The pedal must be slightly sinful.

* * *

Playing a fugue, the pianist made the main subject to reiterate 'I' instead of 'we.' The fugue's subject is the root of the composition but I want to feast on the fruits, not just the root.

Words can deceive, actions mislead, fame cloud genuineness, but even the most skillful performance will not conceal from the experienced ear the performer's weaknesses.

To play nobly while being an ignoble person is impossible, for art is behavior.

'Theater of Music'

The concert platform is not a pulpit, not a stage or arena. It is a set for the theater of music. This definition neither belittles music nor elevates theater. It reminds that the theatrical quality constitutes a very important aspect of musical performance — visibility (the gesticulation, movements), changing lighting (the sound bright or dull, blinding or somber), monologues, dialogues, ensembles (polyphony), and, finally, the musical actor — the person of the performer.

The performer has to master the art of reincarnation; then monotonous monologue turns into lively dialogue.

A characteristic rhythm should not show up in body motions but has to take its source in mental representations of such motions.

Don't restrain movements of the hands but instead make them more varied: they are not unlike a hypnotist's passes, and the performer's power over the music and the audience depends on them.

Facial mimics also has its analog in music: the mimics of intonation. Startling example — eight almost visible intonational transformations in the 15-bar Chopin's Prelude in A.

It is wrong to play a tragedy while gesticulating a comedy; it is wrong to play Prokofiev while gesticulating Mendelsohn.

In imitating flute on the piano, don't sit in the 'double-bass position.'

Art knows many ways to capture the soul. It invades, penetrates, warms up and freezes, pierces, wounds and heals, troubles and calms down. And all these is entrusted to you, pianist.

Playing something joyful, be joyous: such is the necessary make-up of the soul.

The true artist starts a concert not with the first sounds of music but with what precedes them — the last, most important, silence.

Performers, like painters, specialize in graphics, portrait, landscape, battle scenes or seascape; they work with the tone pencil, a colorful sound palette, pedalless watercolors, massive-pedal oils. Unfortunately, in the performing arts one too often encounters masters of... still life.

On Tempo

The metronome is the apparatus for cutting music into even slices. Poor metronome: it is doomed never to know *rubato*.

If the metronome figure does not agree with your characteristics as a musician, search for your own tempo which is favorable to you and does not distort the composition. This may injure the composer's pride but will do good to the presentation of his work.

The wind of performance can and sometimes must sway the tempo of the piece. Beware of both calm and hurricane.

Some musicians handle the tempo like diligent engineers of locomotives. They begin a piece gradually gaining the tempo and finish it with a prolonged, panting *ritardando*.

In our era of unbridled accelerations preserve proud patience.

A hastiness widespread among students cannot be eliminated by such incantations as 'don't rush,' 'one-two' etc. Haste is a consequence; one has to single out and eliminate the cause. Among many possible causes pride is the most repulsive.

Sonata *allegro* must be played in a uniform tempo — unless you fail to find the variety of necessary deviations from it.

Uniformity of tempos is a stubborn prejudice, sanctuary of the righteous. To them Beethoven's Rondos are a merry-go-round rotating with boring constancy. How can they comprehend this circle of temptations in which there is no place for constancy!

Absolute uniformity of the tempo is a sad destiny of the street-organ.

The pianist possessed such a power of suggestion that, playing a piece two or three times slower than commonly accepted and, perhaps, even intended by the composer, he managed to keep hold of the audience. His naive admirers picked up this tempo lacking his suggestive power. The package turned out to be in a sense incomplete.

Don't repeat mistakes of especially gifted musicians; learn to commit mistakes independently and to the extent of your abilities.

* * *

The hands of this pianist behave on the piano keyboard as if it were a typewriter. Inspiration is minimal but precision is maximal.

It's not good when the fingers treat the piano keyboard like the hammer does the anvil. But having so severy condemned this similarity, it is appropriate to indicate what kind of relationships we consider worth imitating: those of the swimmer and the water. The swimmer now moves on the surface, then dives to the very bottom, now gliding under the suface, then as if hovering above it. The miracle requires that under the fingers the keyboard's hard body has acquired the elastic penetrability similar to the aqueous surface.

Fingering is a memory device.

'Comfortable fingering' suggests cosiness and tranquility whereas fingering is called to perform functions which are restless, responsible and varied; a fingering skillfully devised and fixed securely guards the memory against dangerous contingencies; a clever fingering creates pre-planned difficulties for the piece to triumph in performance; a foreseeing one puts braking obstacles in the fingers' way; a deft one redistributes texture and performs reasonable textural abbreviations; finally, a sensitive one responds to the calls of tone imagination — vibrato, echo, soundless and repeated touches of the keyboard, etc. Bad fingering, like tongue-tiedness, reflects muddy thoughts, good fingering is eloquent.

For the flutter of your soul to reach the listener's ear in piano-pianissimo, tense the tips of your fingers and, yes!.. of your belly.

The tip of the finger is a meteor falling onto the keyboard.

Play Mozart with rounded attacking fingers, play Chopin with crawling snakish ones.

My lessons with students can be focused on the pedal, the harmony, the polyphony, the fingering etc. Directing a student's attention as if to the pedal only, I invite him to take notice of the harmonic events in the piece, the polyphonic structure, the development of the melodic line — in other words, I remind him of just what has to be listened to, heard, and understood. Even the seemingly boring 'fingering lesson' serves the same purpose. The links of a learning process are inseparable. Such 'monolessons' are born out of the desire to give to the student an impression of working on a single task in order for him to solve many — to supply him with a single key instead of a frightening bundle of keys.

On the Rest

Eternal question — relationships between the rest and the pedal: to press or release? I would like to answer it with a question: tell me please, when talking, do you leave your mouth open or close it during a pause?

The rest is meaningful and expressive if and when it is logically correct. Logical precision almost always disproves arithmetic claims.

The rest is a soundless texture. Not only it 'exists' in time but also is performed by the hands — with an apogee and a perigee, horizontal deviations and other expressive means peculiar to it. This gives the rest a right to demand to be learned as well.

In Chopin's music even the rests often actively participate in legato.

The word 'rest' is an ill-chosen paradoxical term for a multitude of binding and cementing forces in music.

Don't cut the durations surrounding a rest with arithmetic scissors: let them fade and emerge naturally.

The rest is not a guillotine for the pedal.

A performer's silliness is nowhere else as obvious as it is in a rest.

* * *

Abandon in performance should abandon nothing.

In immoderate use of *diminuendo* there is something of the annoying politeness of the Chinese.

Time in music is an element of style. With the tempo and the metronome indications identical, the time in Beethoven differs from that in Schubert, Bach from Mozart, Prokofiev from Shostakovich, etc. Pianist's relationships with time are intimate. It is within his powers to prolong a beautiful moment or to shorten an overclouded one.

A good pianist finds proper supports — the chair's edge, a comfortable position of the body, the left leg moved to the side, etc. A bad pianist looks for and finds something to hang on: his fingers are glued to the keyboard and his feet to the pedals, he presses his knees against the piano box and his spine to the back of the chair.

Overwhelmed with inspiration, at a critical moment the pianist forgot to tilt the torso to the right and shift the left leg back. By taking advantage of this omission furies of forgetfulness dethroned inspiration and seized the power.

Pianist! Move your left leg father away from the left pedal and place your weight on your fingers. The torso then will have the freedom to maneuver to the right and to the left.

We, pianists, are not like Archimedes: we cannot cope with only one point of support.

To Teachers

Piano teachers! Begin not with positioning of the fingers but with positioning of the soul: it is well known that it abides in the tiny tips of pianist's fingers.

Teachers are liberators: they always free something in their pupils. Thanks to them. But, for God's sake, beware of their liberating attempts at the tips of your ten fingers.

The performer wants his hands relaxed but to the performed this only does harm. Performance must be electrified and this requires tension. Instead of freeing the player from tension, one should transfer it to the locations most favorable to both the music and the hands.

In times past one could often hear about positioning of hands, but only one who played for a long time learns to concern himself not with 'positioning' but with varying comfort for the hands which obeys the dictates of age.

Eloquent teachers! Do not exercise your eloquence in your class when speaking on the beautiful: delight in the beautiful and don't bother about the beauty of your delight.

I pity the teacher whom a pupil has never reproached for being inconsistent: 'at the last lesson you spoke something directly opposite — what is the truth?' Such pupil used to believe that the truth has been found once and for all and rests in the teacher's balding or greying head. And such a teacher doesn't know that in the arts a head full of truths is a cemetery of ideas where eternal rest reigns.

The teacher that plays in class too much produces more parodists than artists.

On Imagination

Train your imagination.

Trying to wake up imagination is useless: wakened, it falls asleep again. One has to demand imagination as we demand scales, etudes, polyphony. Then it will have no time to sleep.

Having discovered in class that a student's enthusiasm had suffered clinical death, I take urgent measures for its reanimation. I begin with an artificial animation. If successful, it not only vivifies but also transforms — directs to new goals and at the same time suggests the best ways for achieving them. This spares some of the teacher's efforts: the many disparate efforts give way to one — monolithic and... exhausting.

It's easy to say: 'flights of fantasy.' But if you had known how much crawling and climbing precedes this risky flight and how often accidents happen, you would had paid due respect to the courage of fantasy.

Art is an unending war between imagination and reasoning.

Interpretation has its limits: distortion.

On Rhythm

It is easy to make rhythm stupid. One example is aerobics.

Rhythm as a noun is worthless: it lives on account of adjectives.

In fact, rhythm is content with just one adjective: flexible.

The slower the flow of a piece is, the more watchful should be its rhythmic pulse.

Rubato — a measure of intelligence which shows Philistine at its lowest point.

Free tempo *(tempo rubato)* is free only in the choice of limitations.

Poets err with their pretty cliches: 'regular rumbling of the wheels,' 'regular hiss of the tide.' They are unaware that the charming feature of the latter is precisely the absence of regularity.

Style is the lawmaker for the times: rhythm its executive.

* * *

Sense of measure is not a matter of selection.

The merit of 'cassette music' is in its angelic impeccability. The advantage of live performance lies in its sinful unpredictability.

Schumann is a continuous expectation of the unexpected.

Performers of the 'frozen' text.

Vanguard will be justly assessed by the *après*-guard.

Cassettes, cassettes — prison cells of spirit.

Absolute faultlessness is a prerogative of robots and maniacs.

Nothing so removes performance from perfection as the approximate.

Preparation for competitions — a special task of teacher-cosmetologists.

Honors, awards — collect them like butterflies; those are also pinned down.

The genius Einstein, the author of the relativity theory, created the perfect theory of attitude towards Mozart by saying: 'if a nuclear conflict breaks out there will be no one to listen to Mozart.'

The teacher teaches that which he knows he is supposed to teach.

Climbing up the mountain of his age, the teacher discovered a multitude of rubble heaps, avalanches, and abysses created by his tireless efforts.

On the Attitude Towards the Text

The abundance of embellishments in the music of Bach, Chopin — an excellent solid material for dissertations but a heavy burden for the performers and contemporary listeners. A sense of modernity, mercy and prudence does not allow us, without doing harm to the music, to save on embellishments.

Sparse dynamic indications of the classics — plentiful food for interpretations. Abundant indications of contemporary authors — ready-made pill of interpretation.

The amazing imperfection and approximate character of musical notation are a great luck for music. To the wise it opens wide vistas; to the stupid — closes them.

Textual paucity and carelessness of ancient composers proceeded from two considerations: the clever one will develop and embellish the text, while the stupid will have less opportunity to distort it.

How long one has to live in order to come to the conclusion that musical notation — all that arithmetic of rests, subdivisions, countless remarks — is but a feeble attempt to explain the inexplicable. Durations require faith but not blind obedience.

Some sciences are "precise." How fortunate that art escapes such a destiny!

Music needs arithmetic as an imprecise science.

* * *

The harm from canonizations is well known, but only teachers know the full extent of the damage being done to the young generation by swarms of reviewers whose exaltation and ignorance sometimes border on insanity.

It is easy to emphasize, it is difficult to distribute.

In the arts one craves for satisfaction but must be content with bliss.

People talk of an artist's progress even when the artist merely marks time.

Conciseness is a way to extend one's life.

Nothing is wider than narrowness of interest.

Be able to hear what you listen to.

Inspiration is the crown of craftsmanship.

Those unable to distinguish between smile and laughter, sadness and longing, fear and bravery in music shouldn't perform it.

Know how to determine correctly the music's temperature — scorching, warm, cool, cold, icy. This ability will help you to choose the appropriate sound attire.

The piano sound has amazing potentials. One can ignite and extinguish it. It blazes and smolders. It soars like a rocket leaving behind but a pedal trace. It flows and boils. Yet with all these it is not water or fire, but sound.

Don't resort to artificial lighting: music is not a fountain.

Make yourself play the C major scale without any contrivances of tempo and dynamics, with an even tone:
1) volitional
2) slack (sic!)
3) imperious
4) humble
5) mournful
6) jubilant
7) trembling
8) sharp
9) whispering
10) yelling — but not singing: on this we labor to our heart's content.

* * *

Strong conviction in capable of destroying any prejudice. The proof — Glenn Gould.

Gould did not discover Bach; it was Bach who discovered Gould. How stingy Bach was with discoveries!

On Bach's blueprints it is possible to build a cathedral of St.Peter as well as a shack — depending on the builder's capacities. Beethoven, on the other hand, calculated his cathedrals down to the minutest detail himself and any attempt to reconstruct them is harmful. Gould's attempt to reconstruct tempos in Bach and Beethoven irrefutably proves both the former and the latter.

The day after a concert I feel sorry that I hadn't learnt yesterday that which I learned today. What then should the poor immortal records feel?!

Do not recite Chopin, recite something in Brahms.

Convincing in the arts is not a matter of what is correct but of what is ... convincing. Please do not take this idea as an apology for irregularities. It has no place in the piano class; it is a right of the chosen.

In the ancient past piano teachers fell in love with the French term 'perlé' — pearled fingers. Every 'black passage' ignited 'pearled' passions. Such 'pearls' made (and still make) their way into the orchestral detaché of the *Finale* of Beethoven's *Appassionata*. When the composer wanted a legato-perlé he placed a long slur-umbrella above the passage.

How beautiful was Beethoven's Sonata No.17 when I was young! — fluttering *Allegro,* joyous *Adagio,* graceful *Allegretto*. And how drastically different it became with old age! — fluttering becomes severely rebellious, joyous turns mournful, graceful is lined with wrinkles. Sad and imperceptible the Sonata's departure... vanishing, vanished.

I remember the Concerto in E minor by Chopin as golden-haired and gay. But now it is grey-haired and sad.

This composition is written in a youthful minor, and that one in an old, feeble major; learn finally to determine the mode's age!

The genius Debussy enriched music, brought happiness to the piano, created a new image of the instrument! With sadness we pianists watch how mercilessly the piano is empoverished by contemporary creations striving to enrich music or even to make it happy.

On Symmetry

A great conductor, Klemperer, used to start Symphony in the G minor by Mozart asymmetrically and pianissimo. The masterpiece was emerging as if from non-being. Some contemporary conductors play it 'life-assertingly' — symmetrically and with accents. The Symphony is not emerging but invading like the sound of a military band. Mozart's asymmetry is by itself tremendously impressive. The Finale of the piano Concerto in C minor is a miracle of doleful asymmetry; take it away and we again will hear the vigorous steps of a regiment's band.

Temptations of asymmetry are dangerous and risky: be diligent — take the risk.

Abundantly healthy symmetry is the destiny of ceremonial music; illusory symmetry charged with the explosive power of asymmetry is often a feature of great music.

What are we supposed to teach? — I think, relationships and sense of measure. But why then in the art of painting and in music does an apparent absence of both often happens to be victorious? One has to admit: no pedagogy of the arts can answer this question.

* * *

We ought to find a proper definition for the nowadays wide realm of elemental sound, to relieve it from the burden of being called 'music' and from inevitable comparisons with it. Music is tired of this elemental forces and needs quietude. The 'element' is also tired by its homelessness and by the necessity to prove its legitimacy.

On Assumed Profundity

Ponderous performance of lighter music (which great composers also happened to create) is as unbearable as light-minded performance of a serious composition.

This pianist's playing has *always* been grave; however, Bach, Mozart, Beethoven were not always serious.

I noticed that musicians exposing a special predisposition for profundity and depth of thought are often entirely devoid of both.

Schubert's music expects from the performer not profundity but a fluidity of ideas. This unscientific notion grew out of the anguish of listening to a painfully slow and overloaded performance of *Adagio* of the Sonata in B–flat Major.

I know nothing more serious than a chewing cow.

* * *

There is something sorcerous about the folk rhythms of Spain. Multiples of the usual groups of two, three, four and others reinforce the musician's will and mind. In habaneras of Spanish composers and the brilliant *Spain* by Debussy a slight diminishing of both is compensated by boosting in us the rare ability to be thoroughly delighted. And this is no trifle!

Alla breve sweeps away all the bar lines on its straightforward way to a punctuation sign — unlike two-, three-, and four-beat meters whose even pulsations easily coexist with bar lines.

The witty, elegant, ironic editorial remarks by Debussy; the wisdom, conciseness and precision of Prokofiev's editorial instructions; the imperious orders of Beethoven; the tyrannical editorial dictate of Stravinsky — one obeys unconditionally while carefree, liberal romantic composers often become the objects of excessively 'scientific' private editors. There is no need to obey their recommendations.

On Dynamics

Dictatorship of the dynamics is so strong that to the question: 'how did pianist X play?' one wants to answer: 'loud, soft, very loud, very soft, etc.' Very often the dynamics eclipse that which is most important — flexibility of expressive intonation which knows no descrtiptive props, only logical ones.

The pianist's temperament gets attention from a double *forte* on as if it is measured with some kind of a dynamic thermometer... A temperament makes itself felt in the intensity (energy) of thought, in the challenging features of performance, in the keenness of characterizations, in the courage of interpretations. And all this can be discovered even at a triple *piano*.

In the music of Mozart and Beethoven, who exercised orchestral thought on the piano, the dynamics is determined not by decibels but by the specific relationships between the layers of orchestral sound where a *forte* of the doublebasses does not obliterate a *piano* of the trombones, and no *forte* of the strings eclipses a *piano* of the high winds. This consideration should restore the seemingly absurd dynamic contrast *forte-piano* in the beginning of Beethoven's Sonata No 27 to the character of a pithy dialogue — logical and rich in intonation.

We are used to believe so firmly in the omnipotence of dynamics that we prone to forget about the sovereign capabilities of sound proper. Sound itself, and by itself, with its own power can create miracles, even in a scorched dymanic desert.

Dynamic designations are imperfect and approximate! Is it worth striving at a perfect rendition of those imperfect pointers?!

On the Bass

In the 1st movement of the 'Moonlight' Sonata the cart is put before the horse: the triplets get ahead of the melody in the bass which, for that reason, becomes immovable. Change their places and the melody will start moving in the proper and by no means mouldy tempo.

I contend: inspiration on the piano commences from the left side. Here — in the severe environment of the low register, the profound bass, dictatorship of harmony and modulations enforced by the uncompromising pedal — inspiration firms up, matures and having 'descended' onto the right side confidently guards it against the multitude of temptations hidden in the beauties of texture, melody and, especially, *tempo rubato*.

Basses! Protect melody against excessive encroachments of *rubato*. This is within your power.

How beautiful is playing thickly infused with bass!

Hold the keys to all the riches of performance on the piano firmly in the left hand.

Sound slaps are most often inflicted with the left hand.

Watch the 'stroll' of your hands. Don't allow them to waddle.

* * *

Feeling accompanies understanding, sentimentality obstructs it.

Nuance is a shade; in music this is a shade of a musical thought. But some people begin with a shade, taking no care of familiarizing themselves in advance with the object of shading.

Scriabin requires caressing the key, Rakhmaninov — sinking into it.

Bach's compositions stop, not end; they are infinite.

Any hill has a summit, but the ocean, imagine, copes without one.

It's been noticed that exaggerations in the arts often serve as the easiest way to draw attention.

Take care of the salience of *piano* and *pianissimo*. *Forte* and *fortissimo* do not need such care.

Piano and *forte* should correspond to the greatness or insignificance of the piece performed.

The dynamics has to agree with the acoustics like a liquid with the vessel.

A fermata narrows the path but does not stop the movement. Ten fermatas in the 1st movement of Beethoven's Sonata No 17 perform this function and only the last, eleventh, brings it to a stop.

Redeem caesuras, fermatas, and silent bars from the treacherous vises of arithmetic and trust them to the judgment of artistic conscience.

Guard the meaning against the hypnotizing effect of the bar lines.

On Accents and 'Punctuation Marks'

An accent is akin to a poison: the right dose helps, an excessive one kills.

Sforzato — is an element of intoning, not disintoning!

Sometimes accent deceives; it presents itself now as a guardian of rhythm, then as a bearer of will power, while under these guises it callously punctures holes in the fabric of music. Protect it: this is very painful!

Beethoven mined his works with a multitude of *sforzato*. Performers often explode while only approaching a 'sforzato-mine' — merely out of fear.

I would be the first to subscribe to a voluminous study of the philosophy and esthetics of Beethoven's *sforzati*.

Weak beat in a bar, weak bar in a period, and many other 'weaknesses' in the art are indispensable, yet they are only useful if they are strong in this very quality.

Ignorance doesn't know the strong beat in a bar, mediocrity hangs on it, talent controls it.

Depending on the skill to handle 'punctuation marks,' we determine the level of music understanding.

A pupil was playing the mazurka section in Chopin's Polonaise in F–sharp Minor. Slowly and painfully he was making his way through the thicket of bar lines, short and long slurs, the pedal and other indications. He saw everything and everything hindered him. I directed him to take everything away and to imagine on the cleared music pages sparse yet necessary commas, full stops, and marks — now question, then exclamation. And the pupil began to speak.

A wrong punctuation mark in a student's performance is as liable to anger the teacher as a wrong note — perhaps even more.

For God's sake, place punctuation marks yourselves: unfortunately, composers are not taught to do that.

I'll never tire to draw analogies between musical and verbal speech. When listening to an actor-reciter, we pay attention not so much to the distribution of dynamic emphases, rhythm and flexibility of expression as to precision of the intonation and attention to punctuation marks.

No special acumen is required to determine that the reciter who squashes a full stop, swallows a comma, ignores semicolon and innocently confuses exclamation mark with interrogative one understands nothing in the recited text, even if the performance sounds beautiful and inspired.

I insist on the use in pedagogical music literature for children of all the punctuation marks — periods, commas, question and exclamation marks, ellipses, etc. This would make them understand what they have to feel instead of feeling what they do not understand.

* * *

What comes first — reasoning or playing? I don't know: some say — chicken, others — egg.

One should practice on the piano at length: to think much with the piano, but to ruminate by the piano as briefly as possible.

Mediocrity asks for reasoning, talent makes you silent.

Don't feast on nuances: this leads to the fattening of taste.

On Technique

Musicians-teachers have long ago accepted as a truth that technique is a means, not the goal. However, a wrong understanding of this truth frequently leads to a wrong conclusion about the secondary importance of purely technical tasks. Shouldn't we, at a certain stage, see 'the means' as the goal, that is, draw the student's attention to the issues of technique development?

Should we neglect practicing scales, arpeggios, exercises? Some musicians, while admitting the importance of technique, demand constantly to tie 'technical work' to the development of the artistic conception. Sometimes they display a certain shyness with respect to technique. But every real pianist must have strong fingers, and this can only be achieved by constant practice on the piano. Here a certain loss of artistic value becomes unavoidable. However, such a loss is less significant than that caused by the collapsing fifth and weak fourth fingers.

Working on technical skills should be interesting and diverse if it is to be successful. The more mature the pianist, the more engaging this work. Playing the scales, one has to be mindful of a 'non-legato' type of finger technique in Bach and Handel, of the legato required in Chopin's passages, of the impetuous and fiery quality of Liszt's passages, and so forth. When one keeps future artistic goals in mind, working on technique becomes meaningful and fruitful.

However, the pianist's technical workouts must be clearly and decisively different from his work on the musical conception. A purely technical training does not require participation of a special esthetic sense: primary importance belongs here to strict intellectual control and a vigilant ear.

Richness of technique is achieved by a passion for accumulating motions and by the wisdom of using them sparingly.

* * *

The epithet 'seeking' should belong to the one who finds.

The one who seeks in art would never utter this word.

Know how to tell the composers who lead the way from those who rush ahead.

Passing from one defeat to another, I have sometimes arrived at a victory.

Immortal work of the 18-th century was performed yesterday in the wilted fashion of the last decade.

Lack of understanding presented in a pretty form ('beautiful' tone, elegant technique, etc) is bad! Understanding presented in an ugly form is also bad. The teacher's task is to establish a certain hierarchy: reason first (which is, by itself, beautiful), then beauty or, if necessary, 'non-beauty' of the meaningful.

Fearing to go astray in the search for new truths, I try not to lose sight of copy-book maxims.

My pupils! Coming for a concert you may not know what is being written *of* the performer, but you must know what is written *for* him.

A reproach of 'divine longueurs' have stuck to Schubert's works. This cruel and deferentially unjust accusation is caused not by his inspired compositions but by some of their interpreting performers.

The fatal role here belongs to arithmetic. In the Impromptu in A–flat Major, op. 142, a simple idea is repeated 16 times with slight deviations in the cadences; in the Impromptu in C minor, op. 90, a simple idea is repeated in the same key over 20 times; in the Finale of the Sonata in B–flat Major the main subject repeats itself many times in its entirety, and its tiny fragment is 'hammered in' in the development section tirelessly and resolutely.

Editors mercilessly alternate their *crescendi* and *diminuendi*, *forte* and *piano* yet this does not make the longueurs shorter. The secret lies elsewhere.

Schubert's music is like a mountain lit up by the sun. Too often performers see the immovable mountain without paying attention to the inexhaustible changes of the light.

The beginning of the Impromptu in A–flat Major is a dawn full of morning freshness and joyous expectations; the middle section in D–flat Major — a sobering cloud; then the return of A–flat Major which turns now twilight and poignant...

Champions of so-called 'through-development', tempo uniformity and other wise things! The signs look identical, but what do they have in common?

Nothing! Here everything becomes different — tempo as well as intonation...

In the apparent uniformity there is the audacity of a genius creating as nature does: the grass is here and there, the hill is here and there, but who would reproach nature for monotony and repetitions?

Much ink has been spilled to establish an indisputable truth: the piano is a 'singing' instrument. The idea is emphasized by references to the great names of Glinka, Rubinstein, Rakhmaninov and others. People point to tradition and the folk origins of singing. But I am afraid that such powerful arguments and frightening weaponry can and does produce in the faint-hearted a kind of 'vocal shock.' If it is true that music is capable of expressing most diverse movements of the soul, then it is only natural that similarly diverse means of sound production should be used in performing it, avoiding giving eminence to any of them, even to the most tempting one.

The fortunate advantage of the piano and the orchestra is their power to express all of that riches. The 'Princes' of the lasting sound doomed to lifelong singing — how much poorer they are comared to the piano and the orchestra!

Let us browse through Beethoven's Sonatas.

In their pages the share of 'singing' is much less than that which is inaccessible to singing. Once I happened to listen to Sonata No 18 played by a student of a teacher inflicted by the 'vocal illness.' Everything sounded exceptionally pretty, song-like and tender. There was neither a shadow of anxiety in the muted exclaiming questions, nor confusion in the answers! In the E-flat Major, where Beethoven's answers to questions surround themselves with snappily playful and content grace notes, I suddenly heard them lazily prolonged, languorously purring: the student managed to take accents out of even the grace notes!

There is hardly a conductor who would decide to sing the first measures of Beethoven's Fifth Symphony. But let us try to enter into dispute with singing in one of its strongholds, the citadel of singing — in Chopin. Is his music to be sung always and everywhere? The Barcarolle is permeated with singing, it evokes widely known associations and cannot serve as an object of dispute. But what about the Ballade in F minor? Is it right to sing out its narrative phrases? Are speech intonations, so abundantly expressive and true to life, a second-rate means?

The Mazurka in A minor, op 17, No 4, is timid, shy, inquiring, submissive, with its striking A Major episode dashing around in search of escape and a cry of despair before the recapitulation. To sing it would be shameful. Here one has to whisper, speak, yell. But not to sing!

Oh, those proverbial 'new interpretations'! They do not exist! They are either cowardly or brave. And good and bad luck is distributed among them equally.

In our age phenomenal pianists have multiplied to such an extent that I long for merely good ones.

Music, like poetry, is sometimes irresistibly enigmatic. Don't strain your brains! Enjoy non-understanding!

REDEEMED, REDEEMING

Having reached old age, a musician who managed to keep his soul alive becomes a manifestation of the mythological *old child* — kindness and wisdom incarnate. I am speaking about my 86-year old Conservatory teacher Nathan Efimovich Perelman. Here is a recent sad joke of his: 'My life passed between the Beilis trial and that of the perpetrators of the August putsch.' He lived in a world of violence where fear reigned, an absolute fear which flattened people. How did he succeed not only in surviving physically but also in saving his soul? The former was a matter of chance, the latter — predestined.

Nathan Perelman was born into a big Jewish family which meant that he was immersed in love — daily, hourly, all-embracing love which could not have eroded. For my teacher the love and moral values of his father's home have been salutary. But most importantly, Perelman is a musician, and his faithful dedication to music has been redeeming, indeed. Strong inner discipline and perseverance gave him the strength to withstand evil in a country where everyday irresponsibility made people an easy prey for the Devil.

Nothing about Perelman's personality, of this aged musician suggests a long life's experience. He is free — not only metaphysically, but also practically: free of the main afflictions of living — enslavement to money, haste, mechanization. He now lives on the threshold of poverty but money has never had much bearing on his life and art. Perelman never tried to alter his natural pace and during the forty years I have known him he, it seems, has not made a single hasty decision. He is invulnerable to routine and has no taste for mechanical reproductions of his achievements, even in the form of recordings which is so customary to performers. Everything he does is new within the inviolable expanse of his emotionally immediate and direct inner world.

Nathan Perelman lives in the present because he is full of love — it is his permanent condition, his prevailing emotion and faith; and it is the source of the amazing sense of well-being he radiates. He lives the same life as we all do but we, for some reason, complain and curse, while Perelman always welcomes and enjoys every day of it. Such is the benediction of music. It blesses the chosen with a peace of mind and a harmony within the Self... Longevity is given to Perelman as it had been given to Casals, Toscanini, Rubinstein, Horowitz. Like these great artists who illuminated the live for a multitude of people, Perelman lights up everyone who approaches him — a listener, a reader, a partner in conversation. His touch warms music itself. Every morning he plays the piano for three or four hours. His immerses himself into an unhurried conversation with music. His partners remain the same: Mozart, Beethoven, Schubert, Chopin, Schumann. All of them were much younger than the pianist and he discovers in their music new facets and meanings which could have remained hidden to them and only open up to an octogenarian. To converse with music thoughtfully day after day leaving no minute detail unattended is to gain an ever deeper insight into the hidden true life of the masterpieces, to assimilate and rejuvenate their creators' ideas. This is a labor of love, entirely free of a professorial mentorship or an urge to assert oneself. Perelman's passion to recreate life leaves no place for anything else.

Leonid Gakkel

Table of Contents

Advice to Young Musicians	6
Precepts	6
On Passages	8
On the Texture	9
On Intonation	10
On the Left Pedal	12
On Melody	19
More on the Pedal	21
'Theater of Music'	23
On Tempo	25
On the Rest	29
To Teachers	31
On Imagination	33
On Rhythm	34
On the Attitude to the Text	36
On Symmetry	41
On Assumed Profundity	43
On Dynamics	44
On the Bass	46
On Accents and 'Puntcuation Marks'	48
On Technique	51
REDEEMED, REDEEMING	58

For Notes

For Notes

For Notes